raintree
a Capstone company — publishers for children

Little Pebble™

Celebrate Autumn

Autumn Leaves

by Erika L. Shores

Raintree is an imprint of Capstone Global Library Limited, a company incorporated in England and Wales having its registered office at 7 Pilgrim Street, London, EC4V 6LB – Registered company number: 6695582

www.raintree.co.uk
myorders@raintree.co.uk

Text © Capstone Global Library Limited 2016
The moral rights of the proprietor have been asserted.

Edited by Mari Bolte and Erika Shores
Designed by Cynthia Della-Rovere
Picture research by Svetlana Zhurkin
Production by Katy LaVigne

ISBN 978 1 4747 0297 3
19 18 17 16 15
10 9 8 7 6 5 4 3 2 1

Printed and Bound in China.

British Library Cataloguing in Publication Data
A full catalogue record for this book is available from the British Library.

Acknowledgements
Dreamstime: Serrnovik, 16, Serrnovik, 17;Shutterstock: Alekcey, Cover, Dancake, (dots on borders) throughout, Denis Vrublevski, 12, 13, exopixel, bottom 18, bottom 20, Hurst Photo, 1, 2, 3, Iakov Kalinin, 11, Khabibullin Damir, 21, Madlen, (autum leaves on background) backcover and throughout, Milosz_G, 6, 7, Perati Komson, 5, SP-Photo, 15, Suzanne Tucker, 19, Tatiana Grozetskaya, 9, Triff, (colored leaves on white) backcover and throughout, Triff, (colored leaves) backcover and throughout, Valentina Razumova, (green leaves) throughout

Every effort has been made to contact copyright holders of material reproduced in this book. Any omissions will be rectified in subsequent printings if notice is given to the publisher.

Contents

Colourful trees

Red, yellow and orange cover the forest. Autumn is here.

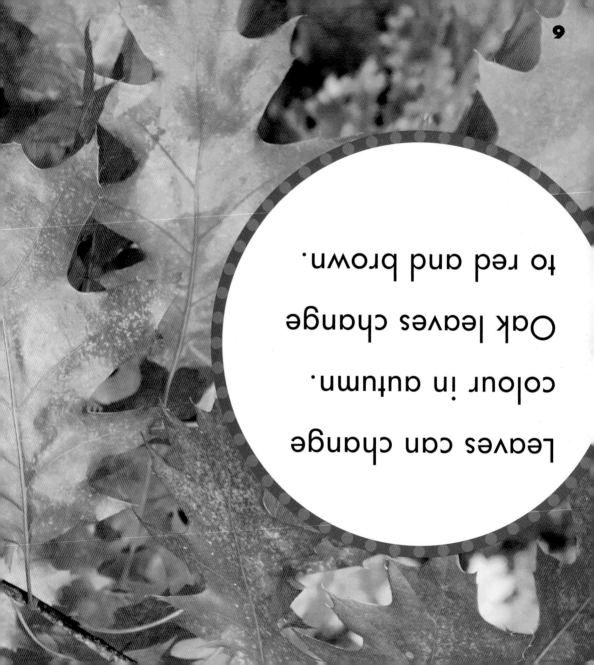

Leaves can change colour in autumn. Oak leaves change to red and brown.

Maple leaves turn
red, orange
and yellow.

6

Round aspen leaves turn gold.

Evergreen trees
do not change colour.
Their needles stay green.

Falling leaves

Autumn leaves die.
They fall to
the ground.

Listen! Leaves crunch
as you walk.

Rake leaves into piles.
Then jump in!

The trees are empty.

They wait for spring.

Glossary

forest large area thickly covered with trees and plants; forests are also called woodlands

gold yellow-brown colour

needle sharp, green leaf on an evergreen tree

rake gather or move using a tool with a long handle

spring season after winter and before summer

Read more

All About Leaves (All About Plants), Claire Throp (Raintree,2014)

What Can You See in Autumn? (Seasons), Sian Smith (Raintree, 2014)

Websites

www.bbc.co.uk/gardening/digin/your_space/patch.shtml
Celebrate autumn by growing and harvesting fruit and vegetables in your garden or on your windowsill. Follow the BBC's step-by-step picture guide to help you get started.

www.naturedetectives.org.uk/autumn/
Download wildlife ID sheets, pick up some great autumn crafting ideas and collect recipes for some delicious autumn cooking projects on this website.

Index